MW01235931

A WILL TO LIVE

"JUST WHEN THE CATERPILLAR THOUGHT HER LIFE WAS OVER...SHE BEGAN TO FLY"!!

IN LOVING MEMORY OF . . .

MY BROTHER, PASTOR RAYMOND M. LIKE, JR., WHO PASSED AWAY BEFORE SEEING THIS BOOK IN ITS COMPLETION . . . "RAY, YOU ALWAYS BELIEVED I COULD DO IT, SO I DID IT." THANK YOU FOR YOUR NEVER-ENDING FAITH AND BELIEF IN ME.

ALSO, TO MY BEST FRIEND FOR OVER 20 YRS, MRS. COURTNEY L. CANNON. WHO WENT TO BE WITH THE LORD. . . GONE BUT WILL NEVER BE FORGOTTON!

FOREWORD

I would like to congratulate Evangelist Valerie Like on the creation of her wonderful book and biography of "A Will to Live". I am truly grateful to God for my acquaintance with this great, powerful, and anointed woman of God.

Evangelist Valerie Like joined the Life Center International Church of God in Christ about four years ago, under the leadership and Pastorate of my wonderful husband, Bishop Elijah H. Hankerson, III. Her presence has added great value, exuberance, and fire to the ministry. She not only serves as a phenomenal evangelist of Life Center, but she is also a great asset in our Jurisdiction, the Missouri Midwest Ecclesiastical Jurisdiction, where she serves in many capacities, one of which is a District Missionary without charge.

Evangelist Like is an AMAZING author! Her book, "A Will To Live" has encouraged and inspired me in so many ways. The strength, faith, perseverance, and determination that she has portrayed throughout her life, is BEYOND amazing. We often sing a song in the Church of God in Christ entitled, "I'm a Soldier in the Army of the Lord". If Evangelist Like were to serve in the US Military, she would have mastered the Army, through her powerful defense against the enemy of sickness; she would have mastered being a Marine, by withstanding all odds of opposition to walk in victory; she would have mastered the Navy, by being submerged in the living water; and she would have mastered the Air Force; by flying above the first, second, and third heavens to stand before the throne of God and have a personal conversation.

This book is so intriguing to where you would not want to put it down. Many of you would read it in one setting, leaving you in high expectation of a series (second edition). I pray God's continued blessings upon this Great Woman of God as she continues to walk in obedience and the healing refuge of God. She truly is a living testimony to the modern-day healings of our Lord and Savior, Jesus Christ.

God Bless,

Rachel Hankerson

Sis. Rachel Hankerson
Life Center International Church,
   Co-Founder and Assistant
Missouri Midwest Ecclesiastical Jurisdiction,
   Bishop's Wife
International Department of Evangelism COGIC,
   President's Wife
St. Louis Metropolitan Clergy Coalition, First Lady

DEDICATIONS

I WOULD LIKE TO DEDICATE THIS BOOK TO THE TWO PEOPLE WHO STAYED BY MY SIDE MORE TIMES THAN I CAN COUNT AS I WENT THROUGH THE LUPUS FLARE UPS AND DOWNS.

MY MOM, MYRTLE L. HUMPHREY AND MY HUSBAND AT THE TIME, MR. MARVIN WOOTEN, SR, AND OF COURSE I CANNOT FORGET MY ONLY BEGOTTEN SON, MARVIN WOOTEN, JR.

WHEN THE DOCTORS TOLD ME I WAS PREGNANT, THEY ALSO TOLD ME I NEEDED TO ABORT THE PREGNACY. HOWEVER, BEING A GOD-FEARING WOMAN, WHO BELIEVES THAT LIFE BEGINS AT CONCEPTION, I KNEW THAT ABORTION WAS NOT AN OPTION FOR ME. SO, I CHOSE TO HAVE MY BABY WHATEVER THE COST. PAULOUS, YOU HAVE PROVEN TO BE THE MAIN INSPIRATION AND REASON WHY I REALLY DO HAVE A WILL TO LIVE!

ACKNOWLEDGEMENTS

I WOULD LIKE TO ACKNOWLEDGE ALL THE AUTHORS WHO HELPED PUT A FIRE AND DRIVE IN MY SPIRIT TO COMPLETE THIS BOOK THAT HAS BEEN IN THE MAKING FOR OVER 20 YRS. THEY INCLUDE: MY AUNT, EVANG. JOYCE A. GRAHAM, MY BEST FRIEND'S DAUGHTER, SABRINA L. DONEGAN, AND MY SISTER IN THE FAITH, DR. ANDREA HILL.

I WOULD ALSO LIKE TO ACKNOWLEDGE MY SISTER KATINA LIKE-LIGHT.

THANK YOU TO ALL OF MY FAMILY AND FRIENDS WHO GAVE ME WORDS OF ENCOURAGEMENT, BUT MOST IMPORTANTLY FOR YOUR PRAYERS. I ESPECIALLY WANT TO THANK MY AUNT ROSETTA, WHO ALWAYS SEEMED TO BE IN THE RIGHT PLACE AT THE RIGHT TIME WHEN I NEEDED AN EXTRA WORD OF FAITH.

I HAVE TO MAKE SPECIAL MENTION OF MY AUNT DOROTHY G. BROWN, WHO SACRIFICED AND MADE A DOUBLE TRIP BACK HOME TO ST. LOUIS FROM ST. PETERSBURG, VA, JUST TO HELP MY MOM AND I THROUGH THE WEEKS AND MONTHS OF GOING TO AND FROM THE HOSPITAL FOR THE CHEMOTHERAPY AND RADIATION TREATMENTS. EVERYTIME SHE COMES, THERE ALWAYS SEEMS TO BE AN EXTRA BLESSING FROM GOD BEFORE, DURING, AND EVEN AFTER HER VISITS.

I WOULD ALSO LIKE TO ACKNOWLEDGE THE PERSON WHO HELPED ME THROUGH THE PROCESS OF EDITING AND PROOFREADING THIS BOOK FOR THE FIRST TIME WITH THE EXPERTISE AND GRACE THAT SHE EXHIBITED EVEN WHILE MAKING CORRECTIONS AND SUGGESTIONS, IN THE PERSON OF EVANGELIST CHRISTINE ALLEN.

ON A PERSONAL NOTE, I WOULD LIKE TO ACKNOWLEDGE MY PASTOR BISHOP ELIJAH H. HANKERSON, III, AND HIS LOVELY WIFE, LADY RACHEL L. HANKERSON; SUPERVISOR MO. TOMMIE M. BROWN; MO. THELMA L. MCCAIN; MY OTHER SPECIAL FRIEND, JACQUELINE HARRIS.

TO ALL OF THE CHURCHES THAT I HAVE ATTENDED WHO HAD A PART IN FASTING AND PRAYING TO GOD ON MY BEHALF, ALL THE MEMBERS OF SHILOH TEMPLE COGIC; GOD'S GRACE CHURCH; WILLIAMS TEMPLE COGIC; JERUSALEM COGIC, MT. CALVARY COGIC, AND OF COURSE MY PRESENT CHURCH FAMILY, LIFE CENTER INTERNATIONAL COGIC.

A VERY SPECIAL THANK YOU TO MRS. SELETHA M. TUCKER, THE OWNER AND CEO OF NORTH MEMPHIS PUBLISHING HOUSE. THE BIBLE SAYS THERE'S A SEASON AND A TIME TO EVERY PURPOSE UNDER THE HEAVEN. I JUST HAD TO BE PATIENT UNTIL EVERYTHING WAS IN ITS PLACE BEFORE I COULD FINALLY MAKE MY MOVE IN HAVING THIS BOOK PLACED IN THE RIGHT HANDS THAT GOD HIMSELF WOULD ORDAIN BEFORE IT COULD BE PUBLISHED! NOW IS THE TIME AND THIS IS THE SEASON! I THANK YOU!

CONTENTS

PREFACE

Jesus said, *"I am come that they might have life, and that they might have it more abundantly,"* (John 10:10b). What good is life if you don't have a "Will to Live" it? A "Will to Live" is written to inspire us to live our life to the fullest. We are to use the gifts, talents, and abilities we are blessed with to bring joy and enrichment into the lives of others, and this in turn, also brings Glory to God. Life is to be lived. Jesus is the "Giver of Life." How then can we live without "The Life Giver?"

We encounter many difficulties in this life. Job says, *"Man born of a woman is of a few days and that full of trouble"* (JOB 14:1). Salvation enables us to live our lives with joy, contentment, and a peace that passes all understanding, and that's the beauty salvation brings to those who will receive its benefits.

If we surrender our lives to Jesus and determine that no matter what confronts us in this life, we are more than conquerors through him who works in us both the will and to do according to His good pleasure. We need a "Will To Live" a life that is pleasing to God.

And the LORD said unto Moses, Write this for a memorial in a book . . . (Exodus. 17:14a)

Thus speaketh the LORD God of Israel, saying, write thee all the words that I have spoken unto thee in a book. (Jeremiah 30:2)

CHAPTER 1
THE BEGINNING

How many times in our lives have we expostulated, questioned, or simply wondered what God's will is for our lives?

How can we be sure if we are in His "perfect will?" Is there a difference? Is there such a thing as "permissive will?" Many times, God allows things to happen in our lives, not because they are in His "perfect will," but because He is a loving and understanding God, who has made us intelligent beings, with the freedom of choice.

Since the beginning of time, God has always allowed man the opportunity to choose between right and wrong but with the consequences of that choice. God never forces His will on us. However, I am sure that He desires us to do what is in His will, because we love Him and desire to please Him. God knows what is best for us.

Where can we find God's will for our lives? Most of the answers are in His Word.

"FURTHERMORE, THEN WE BESEECH YOU, BRETHREN, AND EXHORT YOU BY THE LORD JESUS, THAT AS YE HAVE RECEIVED OF US HOW YE OUGHT TO WALK AND TO PLEASE GOD, SO YE WOULD ABOUND MORE AND MORE. FOR YE KNOW WHAT COMMANDMENTS WE GAVE YOU BY THE LORD JESUS.

FOR THIS IS THE WILL OF GOD, EVEN OUR SANCTIFICATION, THAT YE SHOULD ABSTAIN FROM FORNICATION.

THAT EVERY ONE OF YOU SHOULD KNOW HOW TO POSSESS HIS VESSEL IN SANCTIFICATION AND HONOR."
(1 THESSALONIANS 4:1-4)

Let us take a few minutes to reminisce. Looking back at our spiritual ancestors, we can see how freedom of choice worked for them. Jesus is the same yesterday, today, and forever, so this principle still works today.

When God made Adam and Eve in the Garden of Eden, not only did He give them life, but the provisions to maintain and sustain that life. We have to remember, God made us, and we are to give Him the glory and honor due Him.

"GOD CREATED ALL THINGS, AND FOR HIS PLEASURE THEY ARE AND WERE CREATED."

(REVELATION 4:11b)

What happens when we don't choose God's will for our lives? The answer is that we suffer the consequences! That's what happens.

Salvation

When I was younger, I was always sick. I remember having fevers and sometimes convulsions. Church was always a part of my life. Mom believed in going to church regularly. My brother Raymond and I knew without question that when Sunday morning came, we were going to church. Sometimes Ray would suddenly come up with a stomachache in hopes of getting sympathy from mom so he could stay at home. Sometimes this worked and other times it didn't, but he took his chances. Who would have believed that one day he would become a pastor and now he can't understand why everyone is not at the church whenever the doors are opened?

I always loved church! My grandmother used to tell me, "Valerie, one day you're going to be something for God because you love church so."

At the age of 12, I had my first experience with the "power of God" moving <u>UPON ME</u>. Later, I was taught that there is a distinct difference between the move of God <u>UPON YOU</u>, and God <u>LIVING INSIDE YOU</u>!

I would go to church and see people express themselves in many different ways - some would sit quietly or cry, while others would raise their hands, shout with ecstasy, and even dance in the Spirit. I knew even at an early age that not everyone was faking and there must be something to this. I wanted to feel it too!

I was at church one Sunday morning, and the Spirit began to move. People were dancing, singing, and shouting. I felt good on the inside. Then suddenly I began to cry, dance, and praise God! I just simply decided to "let go and let God" do what He wanted to do. It was an awesome experience!

This was the beginning of my experiences with God. Yes, I could not deny that I had felt the presence of God, but I was yet to acknowledge Him as my PERSONAL LORD AND SAVIOUR! I knew my life would never be the same.

That experience did exactly what it was supposed to. I became hungry and thirsty for the more of God. I began to ask questions and seek answers. I wanted to feel God's presence more and more. I knew there was more for me and that God wanted me to know that <u>HE WAS REAL</u> and a rewarder of those that diligently seek Him!

At the age of 13, I went to church with a young lady named Donna Sanders, who was attending Williams Temple COGIC where Bishop Columbus Williams was the pastor. I thought because I had already experienced the move of God in my life that I was already saved.

Once again, I had to realize that real salvation is when you allow God to come into your life and take up residence. You have to accept Him as your <u>PERSONAL SAVIOUR</u> and let Him rule and reign in your life.

Many people know about God (because of information), but how many know God personally (this means relationally) and have an intimate personal relationship with Him.

The pastor, Bishop Williams, began to preach, when suddenly he stopped preaching, looked directly at me, and asked, "Would you like to be saved?"

When he asked me this question, I said to myself, "I'm already saved." In spite of this, I still answered "yes." Next, he asked me to come to the front of the church for prayer:

Hebrews 4:16 says,

> **"LET US THEREFORE COME BOLDY UNTO THE THRONE OF GRACE, THAT WE MAY OBTAIN MERCY, AND FIND GRACE TO HELP IN TIME OF NEED."**

I needed more of God and this was my way of showing God that I was not ashamed to ask for what I needed. I guess I should have felt ashamed, I was hardly dressed appropriately, but I came to the altar anyway and totally surrendered my life to God completely and fully. I told God I wanted to live a life that was pleasing to Him. A tall, lean preacher began to instruct me in the Way of Holiness. His name was Elder Lawrence M. Wooten, Sr.

My Aunt Rosetta was the first to get saved on my mother's side of the family. She was a member of Shiloh Temple COGIC, the pastor was Elder W. Wesley Sanders. She was always inviting us to church. I began attending Vacation Bible School at this church and eventually joined this church. This is where I spent my formative years and learned the fundamental principles and practices of salvation

CHAPTER 2
MY CALLING

When God saved me, I was 13 years old, and with Salvation I believe God blessed me with the "Gift of Faith." God also had healed me of a chronic illness that we now know to be "Systemic Lupus Erythematosus."

In the early years of my life, I recall times when I would experience different symptoms of Lupus but did not understand why I was always so sick. God had blessed me, and even though I didn't feel well, I was still able to function.

As I began to consecrate my life to God, He called me to teach His Word at the age of 16. I had no problem with the calling, but when God actually commissioned me to go . . . I flat out refused! I feared teaching because I believed I was too young. God began to encourage me with Scriptures, **(Jeremiah 1:4-9)**, was the first of many Scriptures God gave me to confirm His call upon my life.

He also reminded me of the story of David. He showed me how He was able to use David in spite of his youth. Still, I refused to obey God! This went on for years.

During this time, I learned a very important lesson. We have to be CAREFUL HOW WE APPROACH GOD! God doesn't mind us asking Him questions, but we have to make sure we ask with respect of His sovereignty. We should not tell God what we will or will not do. God makes known His will to us, and we simply should obey Him. Our answer should always be, "Yes Lord." If we do not obey God, then we will pay for it. We put ourselves in a position to be chastened.

Hebrews 12:6 says,

"FOR WHOM THE LORD LOVETH HE CHASTENETH, AND SCOURGETH EVERY SON WHOM HE RECEIVETH."

We chastise our children. Well, guess what, so does God. What would happen if we did not discipline our children? They would not obey or respect us, and consequently would not respect others in authority.

Rules and regulations are important. They bring a sense of order and security. If there were no boundaries set, we would live in a world of total chaos. Can you imagine trying to cross the streets without the streetlights, CHAOS.

Chastisement also help us see our faults so we can make the necessary corrections; then we can choose the right path.

God had given me chance after chance to "do the right thing," but I refused constantly. Eventually, something had to happen!

Afflictions

Six years after God saved me, I became terribly ill. I had been working at Clayton Brokerage Company for about two years, when I noticed that I was becoming extremely fatigued. For lunch, I would be so exhausted that I would go into the women's lounge and sleep until my hour was over. I just wanted to rest. The next thing I noticed, I started having high fevers, and no matter what I took, it would not go down. This went on for a while, and then I began to figure out that something was seriously wrong. I started missing days at work. I finally went to the doctor. He gave me penicillin shots because he thought I had the flu. This didn't help either. Next, I was admitted to Christian Northeast Hospital, where I went through various excruciating tests.

One day a doctor came into my room and asked me about a rash I had on my face. The rash had covered the bridge of my nose and across my cheekbones.

They took a biopsy of the rash along with several other blood tests, resulting in the diagnosis of "Systemic Lupus Erythematosus (SLE)." Lupus is a disorder in the immune system. The production of antibodies causing the special protein substances used by the body's defenses against bacteria and other foreign invaders are allergic to some part of its own tissue.

Dr. Beva Hahn wrote, "As long as the cause of SLE remains an enigma, there is no specific and complete treatment. The disease varies from person to person, both in its symptoms and in its response to treatment." (article written for the Missouri Chapter - The Lupus Foundation of America, Inc.).

In my case, I had the butterfly rash, high fevers, fatigue, arthritis, and just simply felt bad.

When the doctors first diagnosed me with Lupus, I had to take 8 to 10 pills a day. The pills did not cure Lupus but did help to keep the symptoms under control. I had to take Prednisone, the most commonly used medicine, in high dosages.

This was a very trying time in my life, but I knew the real reason for my affliction. God had allowed this illness to come BACK upon me simply because of my DISOBEDIENCE! I had refused to do what God had told me to do! I do not believe every sickness is a direct result of disobedience, but I knew mine was. The disciples asked Jesus a question:

MASTER, WHO DID SIN, THIS MAN OR HIS PARENTS, THAT HE WAS BORN BLIND? JESUS ANSWERED, NEITHER HATH THIS MAN SINNED, NOR HIS PARENTS; BUT THAT THE WORKS OF GOD SHOULD BE MADE MANIFEST IN HIM.

(JOHN 9:3)

There are many reasons why we suffer. Sin, however, is the primary one. When Adam sinned against God by disobeying Him, not only did he die spiritually immediately, but he also opened "Pandora's Box", and allowed curses and diseases, which diabolically oppose the blessings God had originally planned for us, to enter the world.

I knew I could identify with the consequences of disobedience. I also knew that God had spoken to me in the hospital and said, "Valerie, if you do what I've told you to do, I will heal you NOW". I knew I had said NO to God. The next day, I was diagnosed with Lupus.

Even after the diagnosis, I still knew God was with me and that He would do whatever He wanted, but I still had to do something . . . OBEY GOD!

The members of my church set a 24-hour prayer vigil for me. Eventually God did bless me, and I was able to come home from the hospital. I was a sight. I was 5'6" and weighed 90lbs.

Even though God blessed me, there was still some unfinished business between us. I still did not want to teach! God, however, was not going to take no for an answer!

SLE is a collagen disease that can affect the vital organs of the body, such as . . . the heart, brain, kidneys, etc.

The symptoms can vary from person to person. Many things, such as stress, colds, and other factors can cause what they call a "Lupus flare." In the summer months, the sun was the enemy. In the winter, I suffered from arthritis. The medication that I was taking, if taken for a long period of time can even begin to work against you.

At present, there is no known cure for Lupus. Some can have a flare and die immediately, while others do not. Since I had been sick much of my life, the doctors believed that early in my life I probably was suffering from Lupus.

After being released from the hospital for about a week, strange things began to happen to me. One morning as I was about to get out of bed, I noticed that it was hard for me to move. I felt numb in my legs, and immediately returned to the bed when suddenly things got worse. I could barely raise my arms and legs. I felt like I was becoming paralyzed.

Next, it was hard for me to speak, and I started having erratic thoughts. I felt like I was dying. I knew it was time to pray! I called for my mother.

When mom came in the room, she brought a bottle of Blessed Oil with her. She took one look at me and said, "Val, we've got to pray, this is all we can do!" She anointed me with the oil. I had had enough! I told God that whatever He wanted me to do I would do it if He would just heal me and not let me die. I really can't explain what happened next, but I do remember going out for a while. When I came to, I heard a "Yes Lord" in my spirit. I began to say, "Yes Lord." I remember gradually being able to move. I was finally able to move my arms and legs. My mind was clear, my speech was no longer slurred. My mom and I both began to PRAISE GOD!

After this traumatic experience, God began to show me things concerning my life, but as usual, when God begins to bless, the devil gets busy. I started having strange encounters with demonic spirits.

I was in such a vulnerable state, naturally and spiritually, that the devil was trying to take advantage of me. God still came in and gave me Victory!

God began to teach me more about faith and healings. I had not started teaching yet, and God knew that even though I had said yes to Him, I did so only because I was afraid to die! I did not mean it from my heart. I was still in rebellion.

There are many controversies about the way in which God heals, and I am not going to be a part of the debate. I do believe, however, that just because there is not an instant manifestation of a person's deliverance, this does not mean the person DOES NOT HAVE FAITH!

I believe God works in His own way and time. We do not understand everything there is to know about God's plans. The Bible tells us that God's ways and thoughts are not like ours. I heard a message from International Evangelist Shirley Wooten one day. She said, "God can deliver in, through, and out of situations." I do know God requires faith from us, and He will do the rest.

God is in complete control, and He knows when, where, and how to deliver.

One day, I decided to take matters into my own hands and force God to heal me the way I wanted Him too. We talk a lot about the sovereignty of God, but when He does not do what we want, when we want, our talk turns to complaints.

I wanted God to heal me my way. I wanted to go to the doctor, have him test me, and then tell me that I no longer had Lupus (now don't forget, I still did not have the right attitude about teaching). I believed this was exactly the way my healing would come, and when it didn't, I became confused. I had people telling me, "Valerie, you just need faith; you need more faith; you need to hold on to your faith." I had one person tell me, "you just need me to pray for you."

I finally decided to go to God for myself and ask Him directly about my situation. I thank God for being so patient with me. He was even gracious enough to answer me.

I understand the sovereignty of God. He doesn't have to answer if He doesn't want to.

After several years, the answer finally came. God told me, that I would have to learn to deal with Lupus, because of my attitude of rebellion and disobedience. He reminded me that for as long as I can remember, I had been sick and that when He saved me, He had healed me instantly. From the age of 13 to 19, I believed God so completely, that I did not take any prescription medications for 6 years. I just simply believed God.

As previously stated, I was afraid to teach because I felt I was too young, but somehow that fear then turned to rebellion, and I began to tell God that I would not teach. After 3 years, while in the hospital, God spoke to me and said, "Valerie, if you do what I've called you to do, I'll heal you now!" I remember turning my head to the wall and saying, "No!" The next day I was diagnosed.

God explained to me that since I had turned down the opportunity for healing earlier, He would continue to bless me, but I would still have to deal with Lupus.

My testimony would be to those who have to deal with difficult situations in life. That not everything will be taken away. Some things we have to go through. My testimony to them would be, "NO MATTER WHAT YOU GO THROUGH, YOU CAN STILL HAVE JOY IN THE MIDST OF THE STORM!"

Marriage

Obedience is better than sacrifice. When God tells us to do something at a specific time, He wants us to do it at that time. Sometimes we miss God's blessings because we move too fast or too slow.

I had also made up my mind that I wanted to wait until I got married before I would teach. It didn't happen that way though.

At the age of 18, I met a young man named Marvin Wooten, who would eventually become my husband. Marvin was very quiet and mainly kept to himself.

One night after service, I approached Marvin and asked him why he didn't associate much with the other young people. He gave me a big smile and said he was just a person who minded his own business, but he had no problems with anyone. From that point on, we became friends, and then eventually the relationship grew into something more permanent.

It's amazing the things that love will make you do. Marvin lived in St. Louis City, and I lived in the County. He worked in Earth City, Missouri, and I worked in Clayton, Missouri.

Marvin would come from the city to the county to pick me up and take me to work, and then he would go to work. He would then leave work and pick me back up, take me home and then go home himself. We used to talk on the phone for hours. I remember rushing home from services just so I wouldn't miss his call.

After a year of dating, we decided to get married. We set a wedding date. Unfortunately, we were not able to get married because I had one of my Lupus flares and ended up in the hospital on the DAY OF MY WEDDING!

We set another date, May 12th, and had no interruptions this time and were married. However, every year for seven years straight, I had a Lupus flare.

Dr. Beva Hahn also wrote - "The course of Lupus is often erratic, with symptoms tending to come and go. The patient has periods of feeling much better. This is called being in remission, but later the disease may flare up again. This is called an LE Flare." With each LE flare, my husband and mother were right by my side. Even though I had accepted my calling, in my heart I felt teaching was an imposition. I was not teaching because I loved God, but because of the fear that if I did not, I would die. I knew my life depended on my obedience. As long as I was devoted to the ministry, God would take care of me. I taught in rebellion. I would say to God, "If I were not sick, I would not be teaching." That is why I love God so much. He allowed me to live in spite of my attitude.

Then it happened. One day I was standing looking out of the window in my home. I began to think about how patient, loving, and kind God had been to me. I thought about how I had suffered and how God still had been there to help me. I thought of the moments of depression and all the tears I had shed. I REALIZED that God's love does indeed pass all understanding!

I finally realized what an honor and privilege it was to be chosen by God to teach His Word! I eventually learned to LOVE teaching!

Pride

Pride was another issue for me. I did not want the embarrassment of claiming a healing and then not have it happen. I was taking on a responsibility that was not mine. I do not know why we feel we have to control the outcome of a situation. We can't. All God requires of us is faith, and the rest is up to Him.

Jesus said in Matthew 11:28,

"COME UNTO ME, ALL YE THAT LABOUR AND ARE HEAVY LADEN, AND I WILL GIVE YOU REST. TAKE MY YOKE UPON YOU, AND LEARN OF ME, FOR I AM MEEK AND LOWLY IN HEART; AND YE SHALL FIND REST UNTO YOUR SOULS. FOR MY YOKE IS EASY AND MY BURDEN IN LIGHT. "

My aunt, Mother Rosetta Watts, taught a message, "Unfailing Faith in an Unfailing God." It's not the quantity of faith we have, but the quality of faith we use.

Jesus said in Matthew 17:20,

"IF YOU HAVE FAITH AS A GRAIN OF MUSTARD SEED, YE SHALL SAY UNTO THIS MOUNTAIN, REMOVE HENCE TO YONDER PLACE; AND IT SHALL REMOVE; AND NOTHING SHALL BE IMPOSSIBLE UNTO YOU."

We have to be sure that we are praying according to God's will. The bible clearly tells us what God's will is. There are promises in the Bible for believers. We need to accept what God has promised us.

God will not give us anything that will hinder our growth in Him. There are times, though, that we will beg Him to give us something that is not in His will and when He allows us to have it, we'd rather He hadn't.

I John 5:14-15 says,

"AND THIS IS THE CONFIDENCE THAT WE HAVE IN HIM, THAT, IF WE ASK

ANYTHING ACCORDING TO HIS WILL, HE HEARETH US: AND IF WE KNOW THAT HE HEAR US, WHATSOEVER WE ASK, WE KNOW THAT WE HAVE THE PETITIONS THAT WE DESIRE OF HIM."

We should pray and believe that we will receive. In other words, we should pray in Faith.

Hebrews 11:1 says,

"FAITH IS THE SUBSTANCE OF THINGS HOPED FOR, THE EVIDENCE OF THINGS NOT SEEN."

Faith says, "IT WILL HAPPEN," "IT IS HAPPENING," "IT HAS HAPPENED!" Faith says, "WE HAVE WHAT WE PRAYED FOR BECAUSE WE ASKED, BELIEVING ACCORDING TO GOD'S WILL!"

Fear

Webster's definition of fear is, "a feeling of danger and fright." Sometimes fear comes because we don't understand. I feared I was going to die. I had read stories of people who claimed to have died and came back to life! I know with God all things are possible. God still works miracles, but I did not want to die!

Christians believe that death is just the end of the physical life; to no longer function or exist in the physical realm. Mostly, fear comes because of what could happen. I heard one definition of fear as being F.E.A.R. (FALSE EVIDENCE THAT APPEARS REAL). If we knew the outcome of a situation, there would be no fear, but guess what, we wouldn't need faith either. Some of the reasons for fear can be not being able to live up to the expectations of others, not being as intelligent, and so on.

I feared death. Though I believed in God, I still was afraid to die. I'm not saying that we should want to die. We should want to live a full and blessed life. However, death for a believer is merely a transition from the body to the presence of God. Our life is hid in Christ. We have eternal life. Death is just passing from one state to another. I finally concluded that if I died of Lupus, I would still have the testimony that I DIED IN THE FAITH! I was no longer afraid of Death because I believed, like Paul the Apostle, that to live is Christ and to die is gain. I repeat, I was no longer afraid of death.

CHAPTER 3
THE TRYING YEARS

Each year for seven years, I had an "LE" flare. One time I lost the 'WILL' to live. Patients that are diagnosed as "terminally ill" need to fight. We must fight to survive.

I had grown tired of suffering with Lupus and the symptoms. I decided I had enough. I felt since God had not totally healed me, I no longer wanted to live. I was just where the Devil wanted me. He wanted me to just give up on life and die.

I became terribly ill. Once again I was hospitalized. I had lost my "WILL" to live and even began preparing for death.

While in the hospital, God began to minister to me. He continued to be faithful. He taught me about "The Will."

One of the definitions of the word "will" in Webster's Dictionary is - a desire, choice, willingness, and determination to do something. God according to Scripture, has worked in us both to will and to do. We have the capacity to make choices and carry them out. God told me I would have to fight for my life, and if I didn't I would lose it.

It was at that moment that something happened on the inside. I realized how foolish I had been. I began at once to fight for my life, and by the Grace of God, once again I was victorious.

The Birth of My Son

After being married for one year, the doctor told me I was pregnant. He also told me to abort the pregnancy. He felt it was too risky for me to have a child in my condition. This went on throughout the entirety of my pregnancy. I am a Christian and would not abort my baby just because the pregnancy was difficult. I was hospitalized once again. God sent Elder and Evangelist Bailey to the hospital to pray for me. The next day, the doctors said I was doing better, but to be safe I still should consider abortion. My answer, "NOT GOING TO HAPPEN."

During the sixth month of my pregnancy, I started having serious pains. I immediately knew something was wrong. The baby was not due yet. I called my mother, but she was not home. I called my Aunt Rosetta who told me to go to the hospital to be safe. Marvin was not home so I called my brother and asked him to take me to the hospital, but before he came, my husband came home and immediately I was rushed to the hospital.

My vitals were taken and suddenly everyone began to rush around. I knew something was seriously wrong. I was still in pain, but it was not as bad as it had been. I asked what was wrong. I was informed that I might have a condition called "Toxemia," a condition also known as "Pre-eclampsia" which causes a pregnant woman to develop extremely high blood pressure. I was told I might have to have a Cesarean. I could not believe this was happening!

I was transferred from Christian Northwest to Barnes Hospital. The doctors did not want to give me a Cesarean quite yet. They gave me medication to control the high blood pressure. Still, I was placed in the delivery room. What an experience! I could not sleep! They had to monitor the baby's heart rate all night long. They kept me hooked up to a machine that checked my pressure every 10 to 30 minutes. Also, I had to sleep on one side, because apparently my pressure was lower when I laid on the right side.

The next day my pressure started out in the normal range. I was brought breakfast and then lunch. I was still in the middle of lunch, when suddenly the nurse took away the tray and said my pressure was high again! The doctor came in and examined me, and then told me that I would have to have the C-section after all. He told me to call my family!

My family members came into my room one by one. They all had encouraging words, but I was still anxious. I was wheeled into the operating room. The anesthesiologist tried to comfort me. He told me it was natural to feel a little frightened, but everything would be alright. I was put out, but I came to hearing the words, "Mrs. Wooten, it's a boy. I did not have the experience of bonding with my son after he was born, because he was premature, they took him directly to the neo-natal unit. My husband went with the baby, and mom stayed with me. I was so thirsty, but could not have too much water, so I was given crushed ice.

Marvin Paul Wooten, Jr. was born on Sunday, November 30, 1980. He weighed 3 lbs. and 5 oz. His lungs were not fully developed. He was connected to so many machines. It was so hard to see him like that, but God blessed him, and he came through. The doctors said, "he sure is a fighter, just like his mom." I didn't know we were as sick as we were. The doctor told me that they didn't know if I would make it, and they only gave Marvin a 40% chance of survival. BUT GOD!

God blessed us both. Eventually, I was able to come home. Marvin had to stay in the hospital for 2 more months. He was born in November but did not come home till February. When I went to see the doctor for a checkup he said to me, "Valerie, there's never a dull moment with you. I have had three cases like yours, and your son was the only one who survived." Though I felt sorry for the other mothers, I knew the only reason my son survived was because of the Grace of God!

Aseptic Necrosis

Even though I had Lupus, I didn't want to just sit around. God blessed me to find a job right across the street from where we lived at the University of Missouri St. Louis College. I loved to work. When I applied for the job, I was hired immediately. I had worked there before in another department. I was even allowed to pick my own hours. The people were truly kind, and I worked for as long as I could. However, after about two months, I began to have pains in my left hip. This pain was gradually increasing with time. When I went to see my doctor, he sent me to an orthopedic doctor. He took x-rays and made the diagnosis that I had a condition called Aseptic Necrosis or Ischemic Bone Necrosis. This condition is caused by poor oxygen to the bone. Constant use of steroids causes the bone to deteriorate. The doctor said that eventually I would have to have a hip replacement, but for now a lesser procedure would relieve the pressure and alleviate the pain.

I took the advice and had the lesser procedure. I walked with crutches for 6 to 8 weeks and took medication for pain. Unfortunately, when I started to walk on my own again, I noticed within three months that the pain had reoccurred. I became discouraged. I went into my doctor's office and asked him to do the total hip replacement surgery. He told me he was still reluctant because I was so young and usually the replacement would only last for a few years, 10 at the most. He asked me to go for as long as I could, but he assured me that he would do the procedure before I would need a wheelchair.

GOD WANTED TO PROVE HIMSELF YET AGAIN!

One day I developed a migraine headache. My head felt as if it were about to burst open. The pain was unbearable. I thought, "My goodness, what else can happen to me." The devil for some reason tried to make me believe that if I called someone for prayer, this was a lack of faith. How foolish.

I called Missionary Gloria Sanders and asked her to pray for me. As she began to pray, she began to say, "the bone, the bone." At first, I didn't understand what was happening and was questioning God as to why the missionary was addressing "the bone" when I wanted prayer for my headache. Suddenly, I realized that the pain in my left hip was gone. I could not believe it. I began to praise God! I forgot all about the headache. I realized, that since the doctor was not ready to perform the surgery yet, God in his grace had blessed me, at least for a season.

Eventually, I did have the hip replacement, but even in this, God blessed. Once again, the doctors told me that I would need another one between 5 - 10 yrs. It has been 22 years and counting and during my last appointment, the orthopedic doctor took an x-ray and told me the replacement still looks good.

Lupus Cerebritis

Once again I was questioning God about my healing. I told Him, "I have faith, I believe in the healing power of God. I just don't understand." I had gone through the cycle of testimony after testimony claiming I was healed, and even experienced times when I was completely free of symptoms, but some kind of cold, or something would bring on a "Flare".

God reminded me once again about how I had refused healing when he was ready to heal me. He told me my testimony would be to those who had to endure trials and tests and that God would give them the strength to go through. God said I was to tell people that His strength is made perfect through weakness.

So, by now I had been suffering with Lupus for several years. Then one day my son got a cold and then I got it. This cold developed into another Lupus Flare. I was hospitalized, but this time my mentality was different.

I told the devil that I was going to witness to as many people as I could while in the hospital, and God provided the opportunity for me to tell others of His goodness. Not focusing on myself was a good thing.

After being released, I came home, but soon developed another headache. I walked from room to room in extreme pain. I couldn't do anything around the house. The pain was unbearable. My fever began to rise. To encourage myself, I begin to think of special testimonies from my mom and pastor at the time.

My mother had also suffered from migraine headaches. One day when she had one of these headaches, she decided she was going to take a stand and believe God for her healing. She refused to take any medication. She went to work even in all that pain. When she came home, she went straight to bed. My stepfather, Walter, said to her, "Puddin (his term of endearment for her) I don't understand why you are continuing to allow yourself to suffer, when you can just take some medicine and feel better.

Mom continued to hold on and did not take the medicine.

Finally, when morning came, mom received her deliverance. The word of God says. "Weeping may endure for a night, but joy comes in the morning." (Psalm 30:5b). Mom said she went to the bathroom and sneezed three times, and the third time a solid mass passed through her nose. She has never suffered from headaches like that again.

My pastor at the time, Bishop W. W. Sanders, had testified about how once he had been paralyzed on his left side, but he chose to believe that God was going to heal him. He said God delivered him and when his wife came to see him, she thought she was coming to see a paralyzed man, but what she ended up seeing was a man healed by God. GOD IS FAITHFUL!

I laid on the couch and thought about these testimonies, but as I did, something terrible began to happen. I had another demonic attack.

I was lying in bed when suddenly I heard someone put a key in the front door and come in. I thought it was my husband. I called out to him but didn't get an answer. I discerned in my spirit that this was an evil spirit. I heard the silverware rattle in the kitchen. Then I felt that spirit come into my bedroom. I felt it sit on my bed. Suddenly, I could not breathe. I felt as if I was suffocating. I immediately said, "loose here in Jesus' name"! Then just as quickly as that spirit came, it left. I was relieved. I sat up on the side of the bed stunned and breathing hard. It was like I had been in a dream, but I knew it had really happened.

God let me know that there is VICTORY in the authority of the name of JESUS! This, however, was the beginning of the real battle.

About two weeks later, once again I tried to take matters into my own hands. I stopped taking the Prednisone that was prescribed to me. Prednisone can be an extremely dangerous drug and should be monitored through your doctor.

Even when you are reducing the dosage, this should be done gradually and not all at once. I stopped as they say, "cold turkey". Then I began to notice that strange things were going on in my mind, and I couldn't control my thoughts. This was a terrifying experience. I had developed a condition called Lupus Cerebritis (which is an acute psychosis - mental disorder). The thing I feared most was now happening to me. I knew Lupus could affect the brain, but I didn't want to experience it.

I remembered saying and doing things that I could not control. It was as if I were two different people. One watching while the other was acting. This was torment. I tried to pray but could not. My mom came to the house with several other people to pray for me, but my condition continually declined. Finally, my husband decided it was time for me to go to the hospital.

In the hospital, I remembered being in one room one minute, but then the next minute I was in another room. I had bruises on my arms and legs but did not know how they got there. Finally, I asked one of the doctors, "how did I get these bruises?" He responded, "you don't want to know." I found out later that I had been having seizures.

My doctor told me later that usually when patients have seizures like I had, they would have to give them shock treatments to help regulate their mind, but once again, GOD stepped in and blessed me, and I didn't have to have the treatments.

One of the torments I experienced was the devil plaguing my mind and telling me that I had missed heaven. He told me I was in Hell. Actually, he was not lying, but it was not the hell he was referring to. Mentally, I could not come to terms with what I believed had happen. I was trying to fight, but since the sickness was in my mind, it was difficult. I was scared. I didn't want anyone to leave me. I was afraid to sleep or stay awake. I felt death was all around me.

I remember telling my mom how tired I was. She told me to hold on. I asked God how long would I have to suffer? God spoke to me and said, "until the seventh day." I didn't know that he had spoken the same words to my Aunt Joyce.

True to His word, when the 'seventh' day came, I became lucid again. My thoughts were clear, and I was in my right mind again.

The church continued to pray for me, and soon I was able to come home. I remember saying to myself. If Hell is anything like what I had just experienced, I don't want to go. I remember God speaking to me and telling me that HELL WAS WORSE! Once again, another BATTLE another VICTORY!

CHAPTER 4
THE TRIUMPHANT YEARS

Migraine Headaches

God had blessed me with several years of "remission." I had not been hospitalized for about 5 years and was doing fairly well. Yes, there were still periods of fatigue, arthritis, and fevers, but nothing serious enough for me to be hospitalized.

During this time, there were several major changes in my life. I was now a member of Williams Temple Church of God in Christ. The pastor, Dr. Lawrence M. Wooten, Sr., and his wife were people strong in faith, and that's why I believe God sent me to this church, so that I could increase in faith!

I gradually became active in the church. It was then that I noticed I began to get terrible headaches again; no matter what I took, the headaches persisted.

I finally went to church and asked my pastor to pray for me. I had now been suffering from the headache for about two months. The pastor did pray for me and <u>immediately</u> the headache left, but it was not long until the headaches returned. The next person I asked to pray for me was my mother, and then something strange happened. . . when my mother laid her hands on my head, the pain began to move from one side to another. This should have been a sign to me that this was not just a regular headache but an attack from the enemy.

I was becoming very concerned. I had asked God to heal me, but the headaches kept returning. My aunt Rosetta came to the house and suggested that there might be another reason for the headaches. This could possibly be an attack of the enemy; in other words, he was exasperating an already existing symptom of Lupus. I never considered that this could be an attack. I found out that headaches were indeed one of the symptoms of Lupus. Lupus can affect the nervous system and cause migraine headaches. I finally went to a

Neurologist, who prescribed strong medication for the pain, and was told that the headaches would have to run its course. I never doubted that God was going to heal me, and I would not, as the enemy was trying to make me believe, have to suffer from this headache indefinitely. Then one day my mom came and told me that God gave her a dream, and though I can't remember the details of the dream, the essence of it was that GOD WAS GOING TO HEAL ME! Mom was relentless in what God had shown her and she told me to get scriptures on healing and read them.

So, once again, I had to believe God! The problem now was waiting on the manifestation of the healing. I still went to church, and yes I still praised God. No, I didn't always feel like praising God, but I understood the concept of giving God "the sacrifices of praise." At church, I heard my pastor say, "I don't care what it feels or looks like, we have the Victory!" It seemed like those words resonated in my SPIRIT! I rehearsed them over and over again.

Everything was coming to a head. The doctor had prescribed 160mg of prednisone, which was the highest dosage I had ever taken. I had gone to a Neurologist and I knew God was not going to let me suffer like that much longer! I knew He was going to heal me, and I claimed it by faith, as I had done so many times before. I told God I would wait until my change would come.

Then, in the month of July, we had a revival at my church conducted by Evangelist Pearl Scott of Oakland, California. I had never heard of or met this woman of God. Mom would go to church, and then come home and rehearse everything that went on. She said to me, "Valerie, I wish you could have been there tonight." This went on for several nights. Finally, mom came home and said, "Valerie, the pastor and Sis. Wooten want you to come to church and receive prayer.

The next morning, I got up with the determination to go to church that evening. When evening came, I struggled to get ready, but I made it. When I got to church, I sat down on the first seat that I could find because I was so weak. I was glad to be at church. I immediately began looking around for the Evangelist. I saw a small, short lady sitting next to Sis. Wooten. When she got up to speak, it was obvious that she was a woman strong in faith. I listened intently to everything she had to say. Suddenly, she asked, "where is the person I am supposed to pray for?" I knew that was me. I went up and she began to pray. . . I suddenly felt the ANOINTING POWER OF GOD ALL OVER ME! I began to praise God, then a prophetic word came which said, "I AM THE LORD, THY GOD, WHICH HEALETH THEE." The power of God overshadowed me, and I fell to the floor, but when I got up, I WAS HEALED!

Arthritis Pains

I had also been dealing with extreme arthritis pains in my lower back and could hardly walk! After I received prayer that night, Evangelist Scott asked me to run. I didn't even have time to think about it, even though at home I had said to myself . . . "there will be no running or jumping tonight," but I chose to obey the woman of God and took off. I received double for my trouble on that night, not only did God heal me of the headaches, but also the arthritis pains that were in my lower back.

Decreased Prednisone

Prednisone, as we discussed earlier, has a lot of side effects. The highest dosage that I have been on, as I mentioned before, was 160mg. I had never been able to go under 10mg. of prednisone the entire 14 years that I had suffered with Lupus. Each time I would go under 10mg, I would have a Flare, and the dosage would have to be increased, BUT PRAISE GOD! God was about to do a "new thing." During this season of my life, I gradually began coming down, I went from 20mg... 15mg... 10mg..., and eventually to 5mg. I was already praising God because I believed it was just a matter of time. Then, for the first time in 14 years, it happened, and I WAS COMPLETELY OFF PREDNISONE! Now this didn't mean that the devil wasn't fighting me every step of the way. He began to tell me that I would eventually have to go back on the medicine, but since I had learned to appreciate whatever God does in the moment, I told him, "even if I have to go back on the medicine, I still had a testimony that I had NEVER had before, and no one could take that from me. I still had the Victory"!

Yes, I eventually had to go back on Prednisone, but like Peter who stepped out of the boat when he saw Jesus, he had a testimony that the others did not, that at least he walked on water, if only for a little while. So, I had the testimony of being off prednisone at one point in my life completely.

Cancer

First, let me say to every woman, you need to do your own breast exams and follow ups. I did my own exam and was the first to find the lump in my breast three months prior to getting my scheduled mammogram. However, I still did not act as I should have. What I should have done once I found the lump, was go immediately to get a mammogram. The reason I didn't was because I believed that God was not going to allow me to deal with the residual effects of Lupus and deal with cancer as well. I also had a prescribed way and method of deliverance that I wanted to receive from God.

My scheduled mammogram was for July 2014. After the test, the technician told me to wait while she went to speak with the doctor. She came back and said it would be a good idea for me to come back in two weeks to have another test, which I did. But this time, the doctor himself came in and spoke to me and said that he saw something that was disconcerting, and he advised me to have an ultrasound, which of course I did. That's when they said I should go to a specialist and get a biopsy. Now remember, through each of these procedures, I was still believing that God would not allow me to get a diagnosis of cancer. I was still expecting the mass to miraculously disappear. It did not! I scheduled an appointment with the surgeon who did a procedure called a "breast core biopsy." The surgeon then informed me that he would call me with the results.

I still remember the day he called me. My Aunt Rosetta was at the house visiting my mom and me. The phone rang, I answered it. The doctor, after identifying himself said, "Ms. Like, the results are in and you have cancer." I was stunned and there was complete silence from both me and the doctor, (who seemed to realize that I needed a moment to process this information). After I gained my composure, he told me I needed to make an appointment to come in to talk to him about my options and procedures. I said ok. I hurriedly got off the phone, came into the room where both my mom and my aunt were, and with tears in my eyes, said in a shaky voice, "the doctor says I have cancer." They both tried to console me, but at this time I was inconsolable. I told them not to tell anyone because I needed time to process what I had just been told. What I learned later, was that my mom already suspected this, because I had told her of the change in the density of the mass. It went from feeling soft to hard. To tell the truth, I was not receptive to anyone who tried to console, comfort, or encourage me. Why? Because I could not, nor would not, believe that the God that I served would allow me to be diagnosed with yet another disease? As previously stated, I was not only stunned, but I was also upset, devastated, and yes, I even felt betrayed by God to have received such a diagnosis.

That's why I've learned yet another principle of faith. Faith does not trump the sovereign will of God. Faith aligns our will with God's. Faith does not mean that we, as the people of God, will be exempt from the trials and troubles of life. We live in a fallen world of sin, sickness, and disease. We may go through sufferings and even have to cry sometimes, but the difference for the people of God is that we have a savior who has promised to be with us through the good, the bad, and the ugly.

The word tells us that there will be times of joys and sorrows, weeping and laughter, but it also tells us that though weeping may endure for a night, joy will come in the morning.

Eventually, I slowly started telling close family and friends, but still was not in a place to receive comfort from anyone. The regular faith statements and platitudes that people would say to encourage those in my situation, including what I had said to others as well, did not work for me.

I went through the entire process of going to different specialists and doctors who told me that there would be a tailor-made treatment plan discussed and decided specifically to treat me. When I made the appointment to go to the surgeon, both my mom and sister-in-law were with me. The doctor told me my options were to have a total Mastectomy or have a Lumpectomy. It would be my decision. He told me my chances were 50/50 either way and that each case was different, and he could not predict the outcome of my case.

He also told me that during the procedure he would take out five (5) lymph nodes to see if the cancer was spreading.

I came home, but still was not receptive to those who tried so extremely hard to encourage me. I even heard testimonies from others who had gone through what I was about to experience. I just, quite frankly, didn't want to hear it. I decided that I needed to hear from God for myself.

I chose to have the Lumpectomy and when the biopsy was complete, I was told I had stage 2b "Invasive Ductal Breast Carcinoma," and that 2 of the five lymph nodes were affected.

Invasive breast cancer means that the cancer has "invaded" or spread to the surrounding breast ductal tissues. It refers to cancer that has broken through the wall of the milk ducts and began to invade the tissues of the breast. Over time, invasive ductal carcinoma can spread to the lymph nodes and possibly to other areas of the body.

I said earlier that I needed a word from God, from God Himself and God did speak to me. However, I believe God waited until I was ready to receive what He had to tell me. For years, this is how God would deal with me. If I had a problem and would have what I call a "spiritual tantrum ", God would wait until I calmed down and then He would speak to me.

I was told because the cancer was spreading, I would need surgery, chemotherapy, and radiation treatments. My first word from God came after my first chemotherapy treatment. I came home and went straight to bed, and that's when God spoke to me and said, "Valerie, the real reason you're going through this is because of your mentality and the statements of unbelief that you have said which shows me that you still have a limited understanding of my ability and power. I know you have faith, but your faith needs to be perfected. I need to show you that the same God that saw you through the Lupus is the same God that will see you through cancer. I am the God of Lupus and Cancer." Now I was ready to hear and receive from God, and also from others.

I received a lot of encouraging words from many good and godly women, but the truth of the matter is that God used three men of God to give me the words that I needed to hear at that time.

The first one was my biological brother, Pastor Raymond M. Like, Jr. who taught me that sometimes you have to <u>redirect your faith</u>, especially if you've prayed for something and it does not happen the way you expected. You don't lose your faith; you just believe that maybe God is going to do something different.

Brother number two, Pastor Dr. Roy M. Stanley, taught me that you have to <u>make a resolution</u> and be determined that even though sufferings are inevitable, that does not mean that you have to accept everything that the devil throws at you.

Last but not least, brother number three, Bishop Dr. Otis A. Eanes, taught me that we don't have to <u>deny the reality</u> of our situations in order to have faith. We don't have to lie on God. If you have a headache, then you just have a headache. It's alright to believe that God is going to heal you, even though sometimes you might have to wait until the manifestation of the healing. This is a principle I had already known, but I needed to be reminded again. He taught me, as the young people say, "<u>to keep it real</u>". How can you say God has healed you of cancer, if you've never even accepted the fact that you had cancer?

Each of these men of God gave me a powerful word that brought enlightenment and truth in a way that has shaped my faith walk even until this very moment.

Cancer 2.0

First, let me say that I thank God for my First Lady, Lady Rachel L. Hankerson. Lady Hankerson is the one who encouraged me to write this section of my continuous testimony of cancer. I call this my cancer 2.0 testimony.

My oncologist told me that cancer is not really believed to be in remission until you make the 5-year mark without any symptoms. I had made it to the 4th year without incident, when after having my scheduled mammogram, there came the familiar concern from the technician about a mass that appeared that had not been there during previous exams.

As I stated before, my previous experience with cancer was rooted in fear. I did not believe God would allow me to deal with Lupus and Cancer, because of the effects of both diseases. My focus was on the problem and not the problem solver. However, as stated before, I did conclude that the cancer (little c), was no match for Christ (the big C), and God brought me through victoriously.

In November 2018, I went for my yearly scheduled mammogram and was told about a mass that appeared and that it was enough of a concern that my doctors felt I should do a follow up test in two weeks. After the second mammogram, I still needed more tests done. I then had an ultrasound followed by a "Guided Breast Biopsy." I was told within 3 to 4 days my doctor would call me with the results.

This experience was totally different from the first time the doctors thought I had cancer. My faith was completely intact. I did as I did before and claimed victory throughout each and every procedure I had. I stated, "I do not have cancer," but this time I operated in faith and not in fear. I had the peace of God. I did, however, as usual with me, go through my usual thinking process. I recalled the testimony of the 3 Hebrew boys when they were thrown into the fiery furnace.

I believed God was able and that he would heal me, but I also believed that even if He did not, God was STILL GOD, and nothing would cause my faith to waiver. I had learned how to totally trust that whatever the outcome, God was in control and He would be glorified! My mom also noticed the peace that I exhibited. I thank God for a praying mother, who went on a fast for me. I believe that there is no attack of the enemy that can withstand a counterattack of fasting, praying, and faith.

The biopsy this time was more invasive than the previous one. I had a question that I needed to ask the nurse. After about two days, I called the nurse to ask my question. The idea never crossed my mind to ask her about the results of my test, but she was so excited about the results that she volunteered the information without my even asking her. She said, "Ms. Like, I just want you to know that the results are in and YOU DO NOT HAVE CANCER!" I responded, "thank you," and after hanging up the phone, with great joy and appreciation went immediately to tell my mom of the results, who let out a sigh of relief. Another test, another testimony. GOD DID IT AGAIN! What a mighty God we serve!

Now, let me tell you about the main lesson that I learned from each of these experiences. I know faith plays a major role in our receiving blessings from God, but sometimes we falter in our faith, and because God remembers who we are and what we're made of, He does not hold this against us. I know I'm not the only one that can say, sometimes I didn't do right, speak right, or even think right, but God still blessed me, and it was during those times that I really felt the unconditional love of God in action.

God is good, and His goodness is not based on our behavior. God's word says that he allows the sun to shine on the just as well as the unjust. His word also says that He will have mercy and compassion on whosoever He chooses. I thank God for both His grace and mercy. We need them both.

I cannot say that I've never questioned, complained, or misunderstood what God was doing in my life. I have had times when the situations in my life seemed to contradict the faith that I was holding on to at the time. . . But God is not a contradiction, He is a constant loving, caring, and forgiving God. As I've said before, He did not deal with me according to my fears and insecurities, but he chose to show me loving-kindness in spite of my failures.

Let me end this section of my testimony with the words I read in the book, "Trusting God," by Jerry Bridges.

Mr. Bridges says, "that the scriptures teach us three essential truths about God . . . They are: (a) God is perfect in love - which means He always wills what's best for us, (b) God is infinite in wisdom - which means He always knows what's best for us, and (c) God is completely sovereign - which means He always has the power to bring about what's best for us".

The Mind

Let me revisit the fear I had of death again. The devil from the very beginning had disturbed my mind with the fact that I could eventually die of Lupus. I realized I had to come to terms with this fact in order to get the victory over the enemy. When I changed my outlook on death (not that I was giving up or even wanted to die), but just accepted the reality of the situation, that's when my mind was freed from the mental torment of even the possibility of death.

I realized that God is in control of both life and death. If I lived, it would be because of God, and if I died, it would be because God allowed it, and I would not just give up.

Another lesson learned, "don't be controlled by what you cannot control." God has told me many times, that my life would exemplify a person who, in spite of difficulties, has learned to persevere.

When people ask me, "are you healed?" I respond with a resounding "Yes!" Even though the healing may not be manifested in the way they expected, or even the way I preferred, God has HEALED and DELIVERED me. I am free IN MY MIND, and since this is the way God has chosen to heal me, I am thankful. Deliverance is Deliverance no matter what form it takes.

God is good! I can honestly say that "thru it all", I have learned to trust in God. God has done great things for me, whereof I am glad, and I praise Him, because He is worthy to be praised. I'm just glad to be alive!

Death was as far as Lupus could take me, but Jesus has taken the sting out of death and the victory from the grave. Salvation assures me that if I lose my life in this world, I'll have everlasting life in the world to come. The word of God says, "to be absent from the body, is to be present with the Lord." (2 Corinthians 5:8).

Thank you Elder Harold Wilson for giving me the best summary of my life through the acronym V. A. L., which he says means Victory-At-Last. I intend to FIGHT A GOOD FIGHT!

I intend to FINISH MY COURSE! and yes I intend to KEEP THE FAITH! Why, because God has given me "A Will to Live"!

ABOUT THE AUTHOR

EVANGELIST VALERIE LIKE IS A NATIVE OF ST. LOUIS, MO. SHE IS THE MOTHER OF ONE SON, BRO. MARVIN WOOTEN, JR., WHO IS ALSO A BELIEVER AND LOVES THE LORD.

EVANGELIST LIKE HAS BEEN A BELIEVER AND FOLLOWER OF GOD FOR 47 YEARS AND HAS BEEN TEACHING GOD'S WORD FOR 42 YRS. SHE HAS ALSO BEEN THE COORDINATOR OF SOUL-WINNING CLASSES AS WELL AS THE ORGANIZER OF DOOR-TO-DOOR WITNESSING TEAMS. SHE HAS CONDUCTED REVIVALS, SEMINARS, WORKSHOPS, AND HAS BEEN A PART OF THE OUTREACH MINISTRIES OF PRISON AND NURSING HOMES.

EVANGELIST LIKE GRADUATED FROM LAEL BIBLE COLLEGE WITH AN ASSOCIATE OF ARTS IN LIBERAL ARTS IN 1994, AND A BACHELOR OF ARTS DEGREE IN RELIGIOUS EDUCATION AND ADMINISTRATION IN 1995.

EVANGELIST LIKE IS A MEMBER OF THE LIFE CENTER INTERNATIONAL CHURCH OF GOD IN CHRIST, WHERE BISHOP ELIJAH H. HANKERSON, III IS THE PASTOR, AS WELL AS THE JURISDICTIONAL PRELATE OF THE MISSOURI MIDWEST ECCLESIASTICAL JURISDICTION.

FINALLY, EVANGELIST LIKE IS A LOVER OF GOD, HIS WORD, THE MINISTRY, AND HIS PEOPLE.

Made in United States
Orlando, FL
21 November 2023

39250270R00046